God Loves Me

Coloring Pages

Standard
PUBLISHING
Bringing The Word to Life™

www.standardpub.com

God Loves Me Coloring Pages (Toddlers & 2s)

Credits
Cover Design by Grannan Graphic Design
Interior Design by Grannan Graphic Design
Illustrated by Mary Bausman
Activities by Kerry Kloth
Project Editors: Brynn Robertson and Chris Wallace

Standard Publishing, Cincinnati, Ohio
A division of Standex International Corporation

TABLE OF CONTENTS

My Church

Noah

Baby Jesus

INTRODUCTION

God Loves Me Coloring Pages (Toddlers & 2s)

is designed to offer options for teachers of 1s and 2s. With over 160 coloring and texture pages, more than 40 teaching ideas, plus a special holiday section, this book is a must-have resource for every classroom!

Our goal is to make this resource easy for you—the teacher—to use! Keep reading to find out how to use each element in this book to make the most of everything offered here!

Coloring Pages

Toddlers & 2s are exploring and learning about their environment moment by moment. Some children will be learning to use crayons for the first time. Most children will scribble-color these pages. The simple statements at the bottom of each page explain the picture and will help you talk to your toddlers about God, His Word, and their world.

Texture Pages

These pages are offered to help you do something more with your toddlers & 2s. These simple variations on coloring pages make them more engaging and are designed to be appropriate for the skill level of toddlers & 2s.

Activity Pages

Each category in this coloring book includes two pages of activity ideas to reinforce the topic. These are simple ideas that you can do with the children in your class to help them explore and connect with the Bible truth you're teaching. Some activities will require some before-class preparation, so please read them in advance to make sure you have everything you need to use them in class.

Make the most of every opportunity with toddlers & 2s. Explore and create with them as you help them discover God's love.

God made my eyes.

Thank You, God, for my eyes.

God made my ears.

Thank You, God, for my ears.

God made my nose.

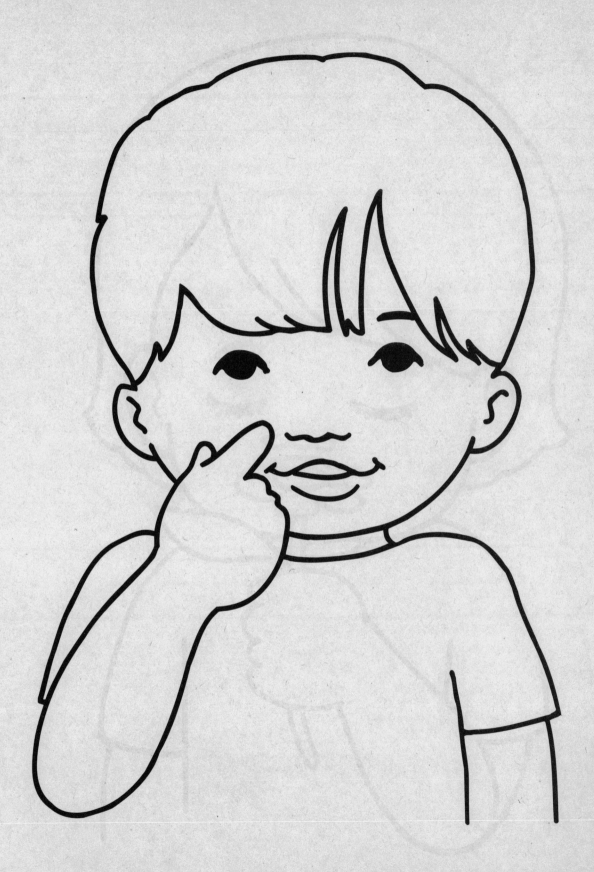

Thank You, God, for my nose.

God made my mouth.

Thank You, God, for my mouth.

God made my arms.

Thank You, God, for my arms.

God made my hands.

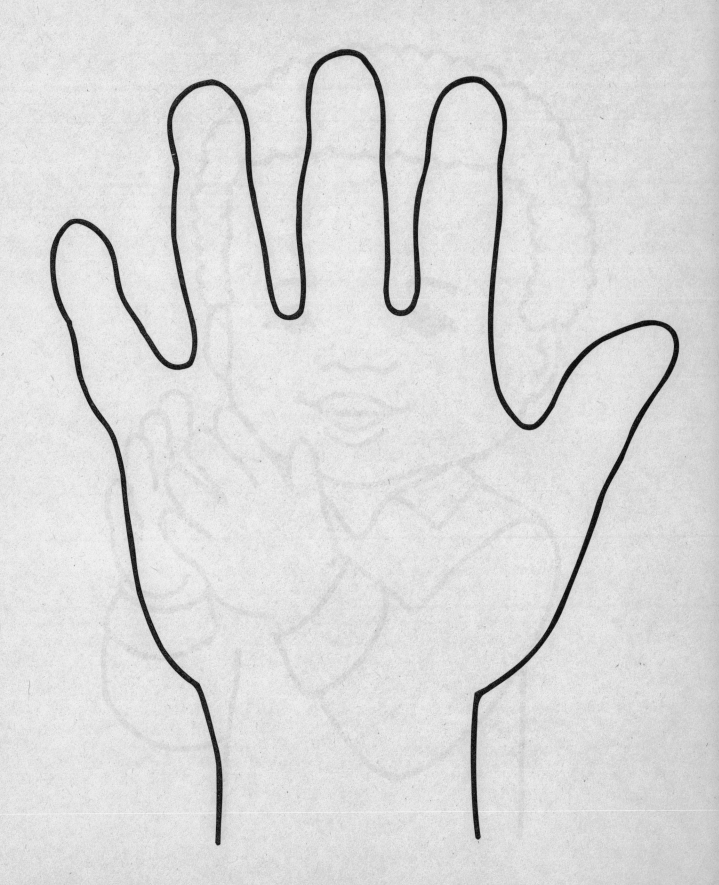

Thank You, God, for my hands.

God made my legs.

Thank You, God, for my legs.

God made my feet.

Thank You, God, for my feet.

God made all of me.

Thank You, God, for making me.

GOD MADE ME

Supplies: Washable ink pads

Instructions: Gather the children and explain that God made each of them in a special way. You are all different from each other. Just like your fingerprints, no two of you are exactly the same. Have the children look at their fingers and tell them that fingertips make fingerprints. With the children sitting at the table, let them put their fingers on the washable ink pads and stamp their fingerprints on the pictures of the hands. Remind the children that God made them. Be sure to wash the ink off their hands.

GOD MADE ME

① Popcorn Ball

Supplies
- Small, lightweight blanket or beach towel
- Inflatable ball

Gather children and ask everyone to hold onto part of the edge of the blanket or towel. Try to space the children evenly around the outside edge. An adult should be on either side of the blanket, if possible. Throw the ball onto the middle of the blanket and tell children to use their arms and hands that God made to move the blanket up and down. Say **Up** and **Down** to help them coordinate their movements. The ball should bounce around like a piece of popcorn.

② Testing Textures

Supplies
- 5' roll of paper
- Pieces of several different textured materials, including: fine sandpaper, felt, vinyl, fur material, velvet, and crumpled foil wrapping paper
- Several cotton balls
- Tacky glue

Before class, use tacky glue to attach the sandpaper, felt, vinyl, fur, velvet, foil wrapping paper, and cotton balls to the paper. Use large enough pieces for the children to be able to really experience the texture of the item. Add other textured items if desired. When the glue is dry, gently roll up paper to transport to class. In class, ask children to crawl over the paper, using their hands and knees God made to feel all the different textures. Ask them about each texture. Is it **rough?** Is it **smooth?** As an alternative, children can remove their shoes and socks and walk over the paper with their bare feet. This will allow them to feel with their feet all the different textures that God made.

③ God Made Me Banner

Supplies
- Large roll of white paper
- Markers
- Construction paper in various colors
- Scissors
- Glue
- Crayons
- Pushpins or reusable adhesive

Before class, unroll some of the paper and draw several large stick figures—about 2' apart—one for each child in your class. Using construction paper cut out several dresses, pants, and shirts to fit the figures. Write in big letters, above the figures, "God Made Me!" In class, allow each child to choose a figure that will represent themselves. Write their names underneath the stick figures. Help them pick out some clothes for their figures and glue them on. While some children are gluing on clothes, others can be using crayons to color their hair and facial features. Younger toddlers may just scribble. While working, talk about how God made all children so different and so wonderful. Make sure everyone finishes all of the figures. Display the banner in class or hallway for the rest of the unit.

④ Senses Table

Supplies
- Cotton balls saturated with scents like vanilla extract, perfume, lemon juice, and peppermint extract
- Small bags
- Small musical instruments
- Brightly colored blocks or balls
- Bananas
- Apples
- Grapes
- Knife
- Small plates
- Cassette tape *(optional)*
- Cassette tape player *(optional)*

Before class, place saturated cotton balls in separate bags and cut fruit into bite-size pieces. Instead of musical instruments, you could record several different sounds (like dog barking, doorbell, telephone, birds chirping) on a blank tape. Tell the children they are going to use the eyes, ears, nose, and mouth God made. Hold a bag open for the children to smell. Tell them to use the noses God made to smell. Let them smell the scent. Next, let the children play the instruments or listen to the cassette tape sounds. Remind them that God made our ears to hear. Hold up the blocks or balls and ask them to use their eyes to tell you the colors. They will also use their mouths God made to taste the fruits, as you cut them up at the table.

God made baby girls.

God made baby boys.

God made big girls.

God made big boys.

God made mothers.

God made fathers.

God made grandmas.

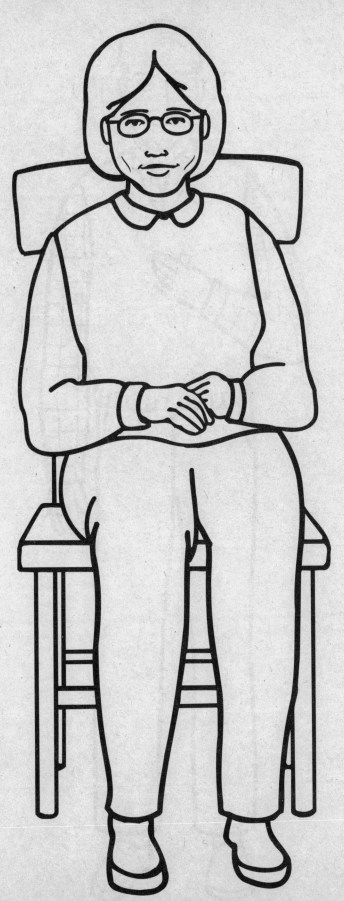

God made grandpas.

God made brothers.

God made sisters.

God made leaders.

God made teachers.

God made doctors.

God made firefighters.

God made police officers.

43

GOD MADE PEOPLE

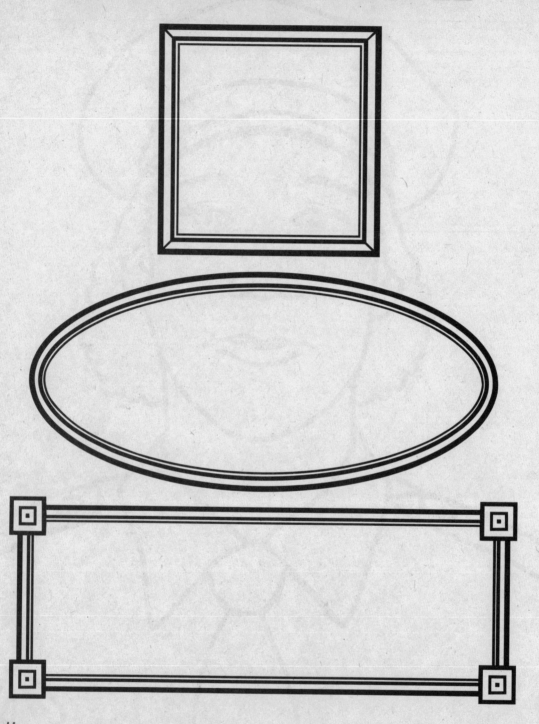

Supplies: Magazines, scissors, glue sticks

Instructions: Before class, cut out magazine pictures of different types of people. Be sure that both male and female are represented. Mix up your picture selection so that some people are working, some are with children, some are cooking, etc. During class, have the children choose different pictures of people and glue them onto their picture frames. Explain to them that God made all people.

God Made People

① People Puppets

Supplies
- Several magazines
- Scissors
- Construction paper
- Glue stick
- Craft sticks

Before class, cut out pictures of several different types of people from magazines. Try to find men, women, children, babies, and different types of workers. Then glue the pictures to construction paper to make them stiffer. In class, allow children to select one or two of the people to make into puppets. Help children choose some people and use a glue stick to attach the people to the craft sticks. While working, talk about how God made different types of people and what types of people He made. After puppets are finished, encourage children to play with them. Make some puppets yourself, before class, and use your puppets to stage a show for the children.

② Care Center

Supplies
- Several baby dolls
- Doll clothes
- Toy baby bottle
- Child chairs
- Toy doctor accessories

Before class, set up part of the room as a Care Center, where children can pretend to care for others as parents, grandparents, firefighters, police officers, and doctors. Set up small chairs, tables, baby beds, and baby dolls. Tell the children they are going to the Care Center to practice caring for others. Show them how to hold the babies and feed them with the toy bottles. They can pretend to care for the babies as parents and grandparents do, changing and feeding the babies. Talk about how God made parents and grandparents to take care of babies and children. And God made babies and children too! Other children can pretend to be doctors. Emphasize that God made doctors, firefighters, police officers, and families to help and care for each other.

③ Helper Town

Supplies
- Large carpet play mat with roads or use masking tape to make roads on the floor Many small preschool toy vehicles, including mail trucks, tow trucks, police cars or fire trucks Preschool toy people to ride in the vehicles

Spread out mat in classroom. Encourage children to take a car and play along the outside of the mat. Ask the children to pick the toy people to ride with them. As they play and drive their vehicles through the town, remind them what firefighters, mailmen, police officers, etc. do in a town. They can pretend to be a firefighter driving to put out a fire. They could also be a police officer helping other cars to drive safely. Another car could be a family driving to the grocery store, the park, or to church. Remind them as they play that God made families to love and care for each other.

④ Follow the Leader

Supplies
- Several baby dolls
- Several children's books
- Several toy phones

Line children up and tell them to follow you around the room and do what you do. Tell them you are going to pretend to be all different kinds of people that God made. First pretend to be a baby, crawling and making crying sounds. Encourage children to copy and follow you. Next tell them you are big brothers and sisters, stretching up tall and walking as tall as you can. Continue your walk by pretending to be various people, like a soldier or a member of a marching band or a runner. At the end of your walk, sit down by the baby dolls, books, and toy phones. Tell children you are now pretending to be mommies, daddies, and grandparents—holding babies, talking on the phone, reading the newspaper, or reading books. Thank God for making our families to take care of us and for making all people.

God made vegetables.

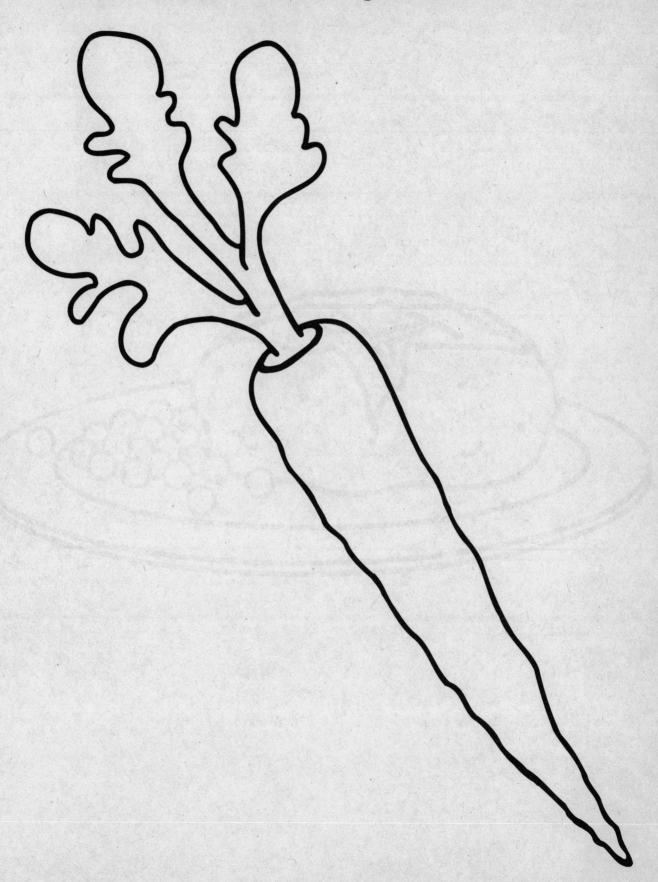

47

Thank You, God, for vegetables.

God made fruit.

Thank You, God, for fruit.

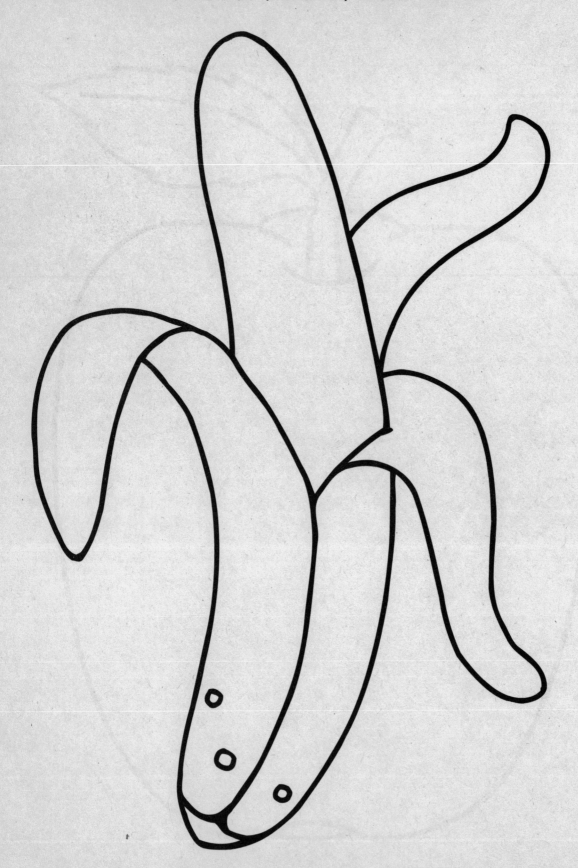

God made bread.

God made cereal.

God made water.

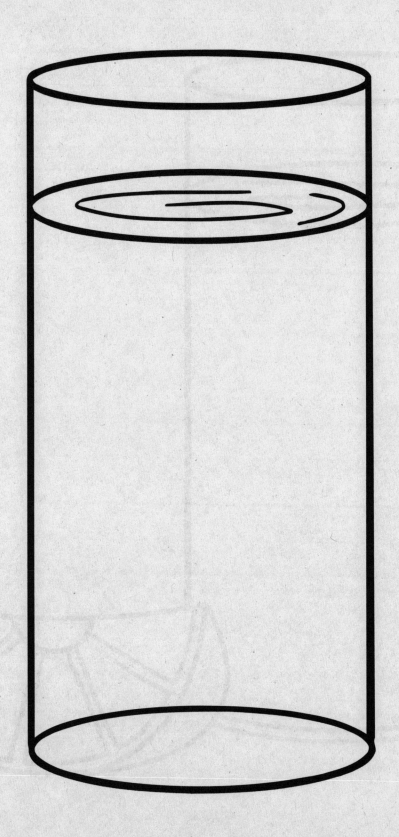

God made juice.

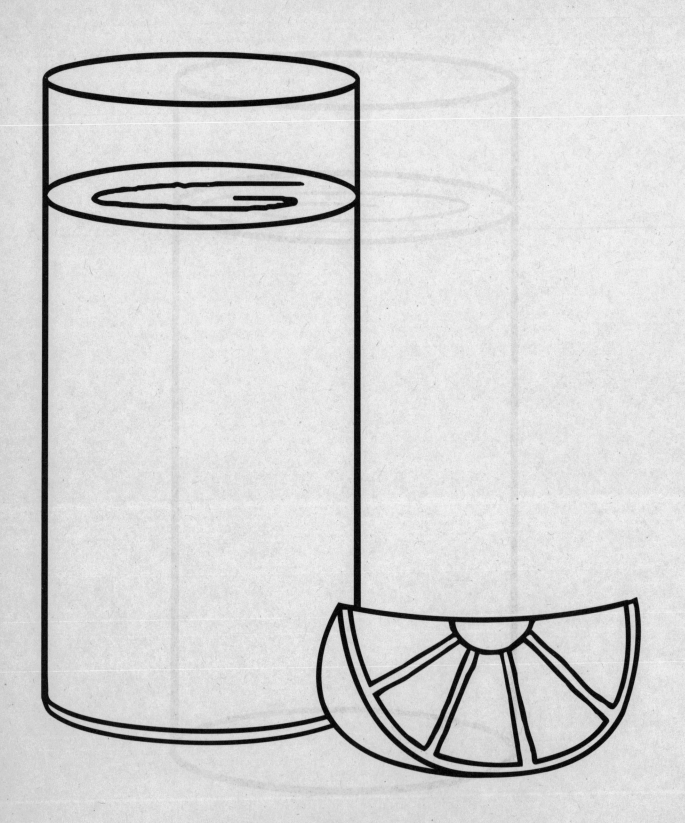

GOD MADE FOOD

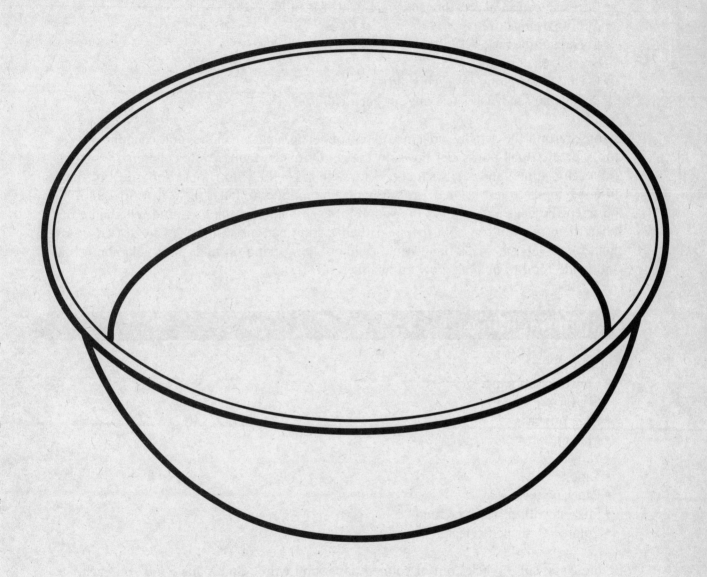

Supplies: Supplies, box of O-shaped cereal, bag of shredded carrots, a few paper plates, glue sticks

Instructions: Gather the children together to tell them that they will be learning about all the good food God made for them to eat. At the table, pour O-shaped cereal and shredded carrots on paper plates for the children to share. Help the kids choose pieces of carrots and cereal to glue onto the picture of the bowl. Remind the children that God made all good foods for them to eat and to help them grow up to be big and strong.

GOD MADE FOOD

① Tasting Bags

Supplies
- Bite-size cereal, like O-shaped cereal or wheat puffs
- Mini marshmallows
- Cheddar fish crackers
- Several small bowls
- Plastic spoons, one for each child
- Resealable sandwich bags, one for each child

Before starting the activity, pour two types of cereal, marshmallows, and cheddar crackers into separate small bowls. Set bowls in the center of the table. While children are seated, give each a spoon and sandwich bag. Allow them, carefully, to choose spoonfuls of the different foods to put in their Tasting Bags. For younger toddlers, help them by holding open the bags and guiding the spoon into the bag. Seal the bags and tell children to shake them up. You can have them eat their tasting bag mix while they are seated or save them to eat later at snack time. While children are working on their bags, talk about how God made food to help us grow up healthy and strong.

② Stringing Rings

Supplies
- Construction paper
- Scissors
- Hole punch
- Marker
- Yarn
- Tape
- Paper plates
- Stickers with pictures of food
- Colored O-shaped cereal

Before class, cut 3" circles out of colored paper and write "God Made Food" on each. Punch a hole in each circle. Cut 2' lengths of yarn and wrap tape around one end for easier stringing. Then, tie a knot around one piece of cereal at the end of each string of yarn. Give each of the children a colored circle and have them put a few food stickers on it. Write their names on the back of the circles. Then pour a small amount of cereal on paper plates and tell them to string cereal on the yarn for a necklace. Younger children will need more help with this. String the circle on the yarn along with the cereal. When children are finished, tie the string together like a necklace. Remind them how thankful we are to God that He made food for us.

③ Growing Food

Supplies
- Plastic toy gardening tools
- Plastic toy food
- Tub of play sand

Give children gardening tools and tell them they are going to help grow food. Show them how you dig in the sand and plant a seed (toy food). Then cover it up with dirt and tell them how God sends rain and sunshine to grow the plant. Then give them the toy food to dig up (or harvest) from the ground. Let them do all these things while you are talking. Then tell them to pretend to be the growing plant. They can squat down near the floor. **First, the seed is inside the ground. Then God sends rain and sunshine, and the plant comes up from the ground and grows taller and taller.** As you are talking, show children how they can stand up until they are a tall plant, with arms spread high. Tell them that growing plants are one way that God gives us good food to eat.

④ Food Hunt

Supplies
- Many pieces of toy food, like: apples, bananas, oranges, grapes, bread, pizza, juice bottles, hot dogs, and hamburgers
- Paper lunch bags

Before class, hide many pieces of toy food around the classroom. Hide enough so each child can find several pieces of food. Hide them in easily seen places where toddlers can spot them. Gather children and tell them they are going on a food hunt. Give each child a bag and supervise them as they look around the classroom for the food. Some children might need more help than others as they are looking for food items. Others might have to be told to sit down after they've quickly found a few items. When each child has found a few items, pull out the items one at a time and identify them. Help them identify the food items and talk about how God made all food and gives it to us so we can be healthy and strong.

God made the sky.

God made clouds.

God made birds.

God made birds that fly.

God made birds that walk.

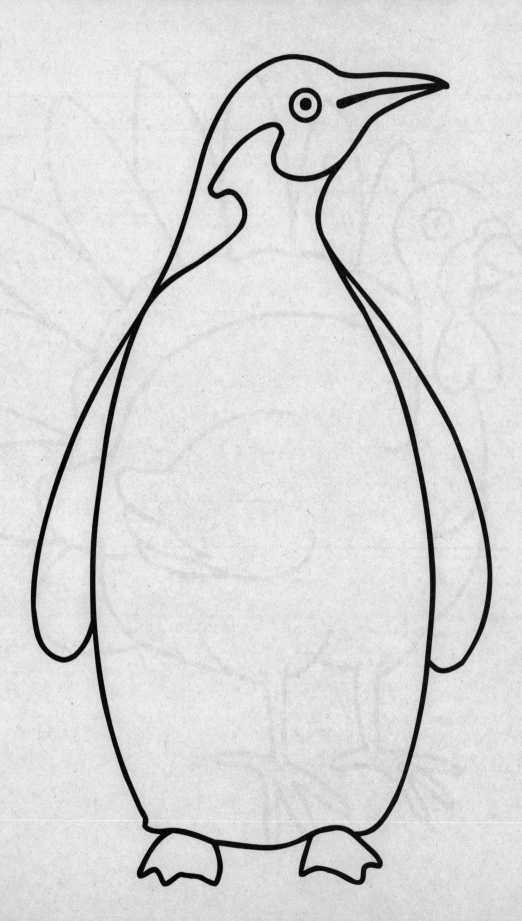

God made big birds.

God made little birds.

God made the sun.

God made the moon.

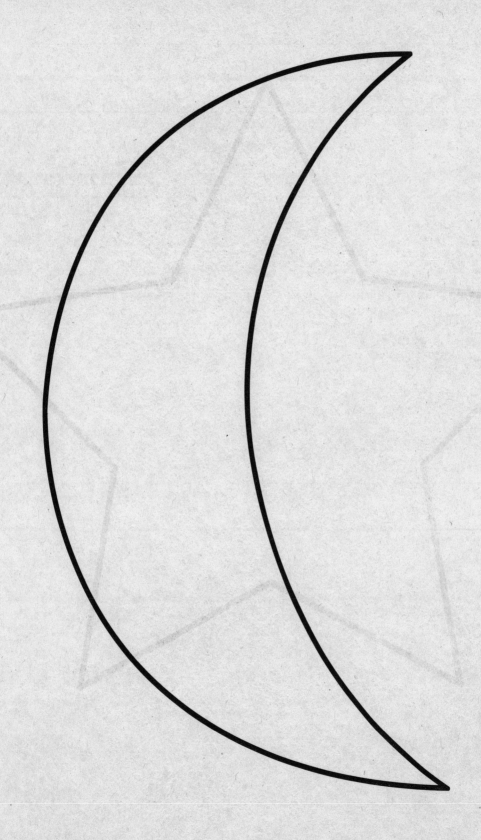

God made the stars.

God made the ocean.

God made puddles.

God made mountains.

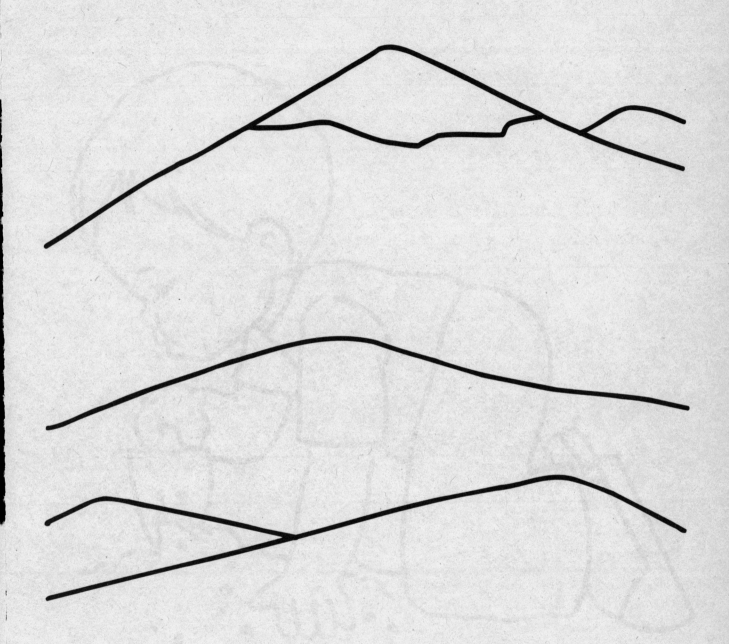

God made dirt.

God made fish.

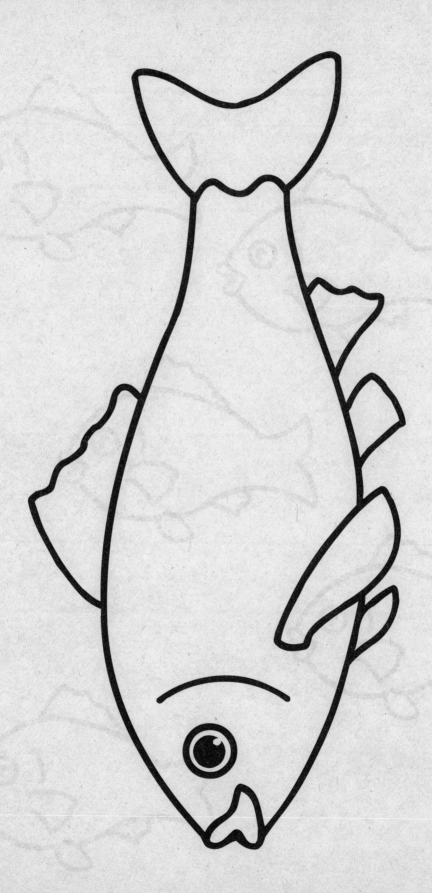

God made little fish.

God made big fish.

God made trees.

God made plants.

God made bushes.

God made flowers.

God made bugs with legs.

God made bugs that fly.

God made puppies.

God made kittens.

God made elephants.

God made giraffes.

God made horses.

God made cows.

God made animals with hard shells.

God made animals with soft fur.

God made animals that crawl.

God made animals that jump.

91

God made fall.

God made winter.

God made spring.

God made summer.

GOD MADE THE WORLD

Supplies: Large crayons, stickers with flower designs (scratch 'n sniff, if possible).

Instructions: Have the children color the picture on the coloring page. Then, peel off a few stickers for each child and allow them to choose the ones they like and stick them to the coloring page. Explain to them that God made the world and all of the things in it, like green grass and pretty flowers.

GOD MADE THE WORLD

① Pond Fishing

Supplies
- Colored construction paper
- Pen
- Scissors
- Adhesive magnet strip
- Empty paper towel rolls, one for each child
- Yarn
- Blue blanket or sheet

Before class, trace and cut out several fish shapes from colored paper. Cut a 1" piece from the magnet strip and affix to each fish. Tape 18" of yarn to the end of paper towel rolls to make fishing rods. On the other end of the yarn, tie a knot around a 2" piece of the magnet strip, with backing paper still on. Make sure that the magnetic part of the magnet is facedown. In class, spread a blue blanket on the floor in a round shape and spread the fish on top, near the edges. Give children the "rods" and take them to the "pond" to go fishing. Have them stand around the outside of the blanket and try to "catch" the fish. Younger toddlers may need help guiding the magnets together. Talk about how God made ponds and lakes and the fish that live there.

② Leaf Rubbings

Supplies
- Several medium-size leaves
- White paper
- Large crayons

Before class, scatter the leaves around the class or in an area where children can go on a leaf hunt. Take the children on a walk in this area, allowing each to pick up a couple of leaves. Talks about how God made trees and leaves that grow on them. You could also do this walk outside, if appropriate. At the table, give each child a paper and show them how they can put the leaf under the paper and rub on it with a crayon on the paper. This will show the beautiful shape of the leaf that God made. You will have to help some children by holding the paper or encouraging them to press a little harder. Let them do several rubbings until they have multiple leaves on their papers.

① Water Play

Supplies
- Large plastic tub
- Water
- Small toy boats
- Small cups
- Live plants
- Large apples
- Sponges
- Towels
- Smocks *(optional)*

Fill a tub with 2" of water and set it on a towel. Put smocks on children *(optional)*. Tell them that when God made the world, He made water for us to drink and for plants and animals to drink too. He also made water so we could swim and wash our bodies and clothes. Allow children to play with boats and cups in the water tub. Help children, one at a time, get a small cup of water and water one of the plants that God made. You can help other children wash the apples that God made and see how they look. Be sure to supervise closely and have plenty of towels handy for this activity.

② Reaching the Seasons

Supplies
- Marker
- Various colors of paper
- Scissors
- Yarn
- Tape

Before class, draw and cut out four different shapes to represent the four seasons, such as: orange or red leaf for fall, white snowflake for winter, light blue, purple and green butterflies for spring, and yellow sun for summer. Attach each shape to a piece of yarn and tape to the ceiling. Gather children under the shapes. Tell them you want them to find the shape for each season. When it's fall, the tree leaves turn pretty colors and fall down. Can you find the fall leaf? Talk about how God made fall and all the other seasons that we see. When they find the leaf, ask them to "catch" them by reaching and jumping up. Do the same with all four seasons, asking them to find the seasonal shapes and then jump up to "catch" them.

God gives me food.

Thank you, God, for food.

God gives me clothes.

Thank you, God, for clothes.

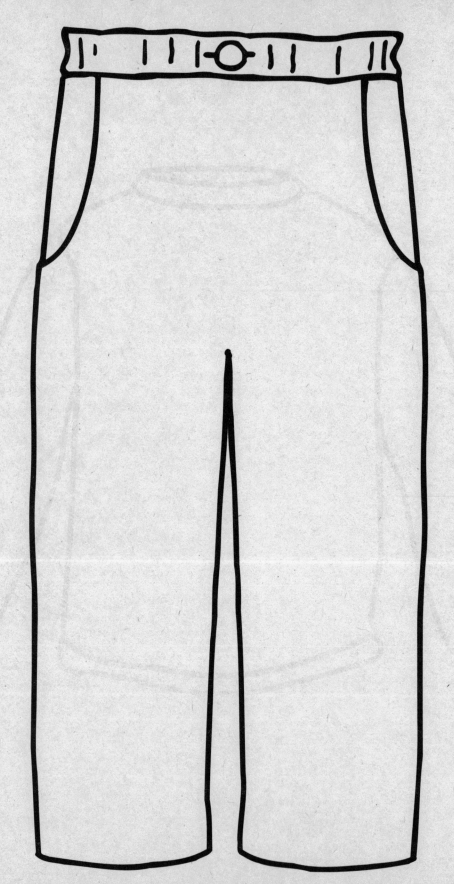

God gives me shoes.

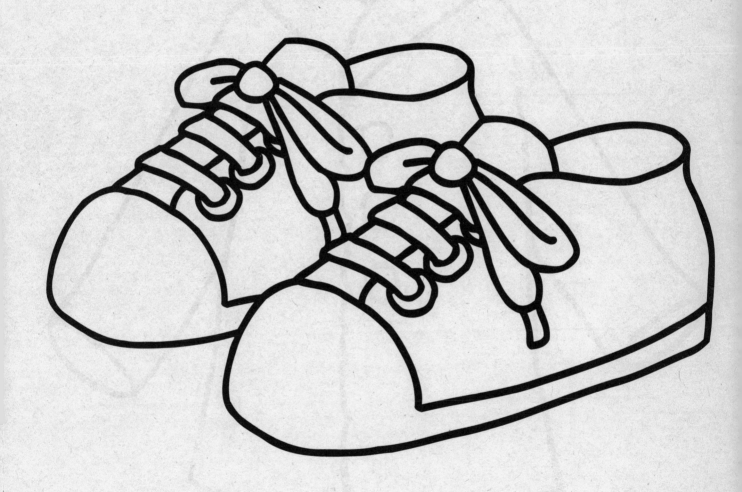

My clothes keep me warm.

God gives me a place to live.

God gives me a place to sleep.

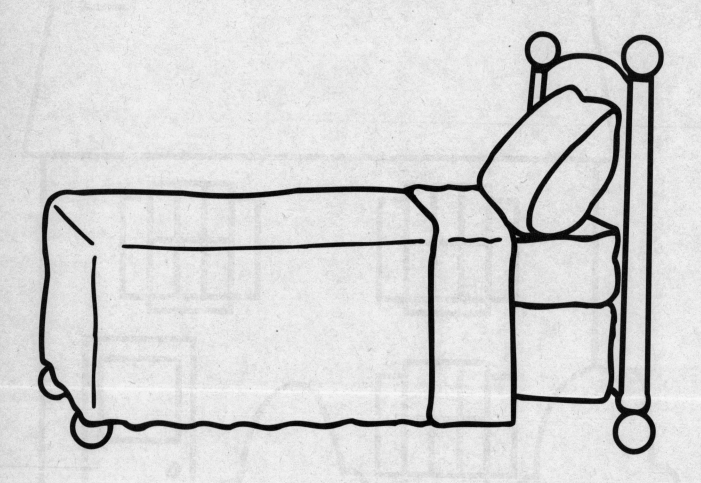

God gives me good things.

Thank you, God, for good things.

God gives me water.

109

Thank you, God, for good water.

GOD GIVES ME GOOD THINGS

Supplies: Old clothing, scissors, glue sticks

Instructions: Before class, cut fabric into small pieces. During class, let the children choose pieces of the fabric and help them glue those onto the shirt on their coloring pages. Explain how God made good things for us, like clothes to keep us warm.

GOD GIVES ME GOOD THINGS

ACTIVITIES

① Food Table

Supplies
- Construction paper
- Pen
- Thin fabric
- Glue stick
- Crayons
- O-shaped cereal

Before class, write, "God Gives Me Good Things" in big letters across the top of construction paper. Cut some thin fabric 7" by 2" pieces to make tablecloths. Cut more construction paper into 1 inch circles. Give each child a paper and allow them to pick out a tablecloth. Help them glue the tablecloth onto the table on their paper. While some children are gluing, others can be coloring their papers. Children will then pick out one or two construction paper circles and glue them onto the tablecloth. Toddlers will then pick some cereal rings and glue them on the circle to represent the food God gives us.

② Feeling Socks

Supplies
- Adult tube sock
- Small objects that fit inside socks, like: ball, block, car, spoon, cup, apple

Put a small toy (that are easily identified by shape) inside the adult-size sock. Show children the sock and let them all have a chance to feel the object from outside of the sock. **What do you feel?** Tell them you want them to guess what you have in the socks. If they identify the object, talk about how God gives us that and how we use it. For younger toddlers, you could allow them to feel it first and then pull it out and identify it by sight. Less-verbal children may not say what the object is, but you can involve them by asking, **is that a ball?** And give them the opportunity to indicate yes.

③ Beanbag Toss

Supplies
- 4—5 small boxes
- Magazines
- Scissors
- Glue
- Two or three beanbags

Before class, cut out of magazines several examples of good things God gives us. You could pick out things like: children's clothes, pets, food, houses, furniture, and toys. Glue one "good thing" in the bottom of each box. In class, set up the boxes in a line. Have children stand a short distance away and try to toss beanbags into the boxes. When they make it, encourage them to get the beanbag out of the box and name the picture in the box. Talk about God's good gifts.

④ Cleaning House

Supplies
- Small broom and dustpan
- Dustcloths
- Toy vacuum
- Paper bags
- Scrap paper
- Small table
- Toy dishes and food
- Play kitchen *(optional)*

Invite the toddlers to help clean up your home and get ready for some friends to come over. Give children the various housecleaning tools and show them how to use the items. Scatter some scrap paper in the area and assign a few children to pick up the trash and put it in their paper bags. Children can also set the table with the toy dishes and food, or help to prepare the meal. Other children could be taking care of the babies while the rest are cooking and cleaning. Remind them that God gives us all these good things and He is happy when we share them with our friends.

God cares for me in the morning.

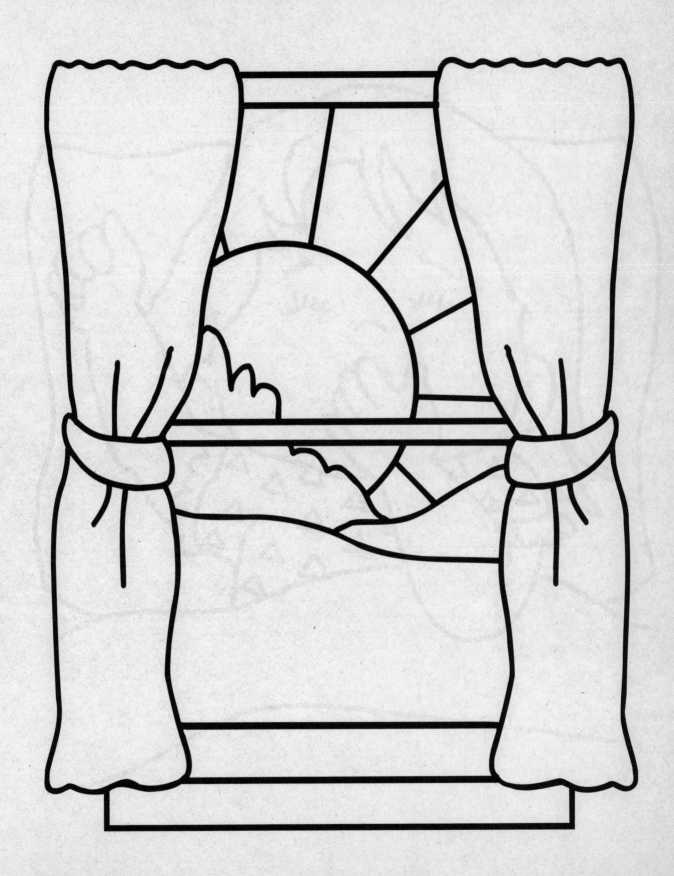

God cares for me when I wake up.

God cares for me when I am eating.

God cares for me when I am thirsty.

God cares for me when I am playing.

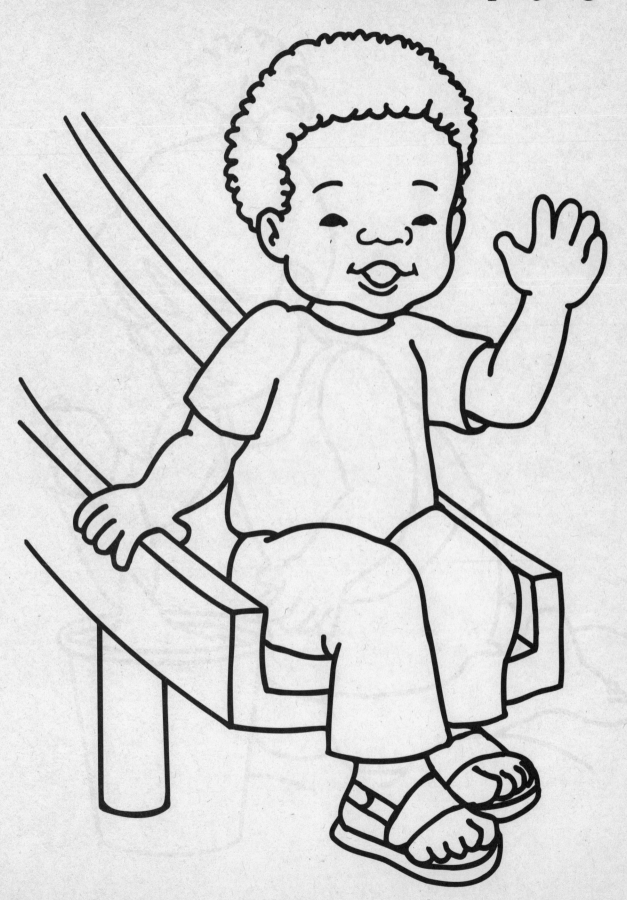

God cares for me when I go to new places.

God cares for me at night.

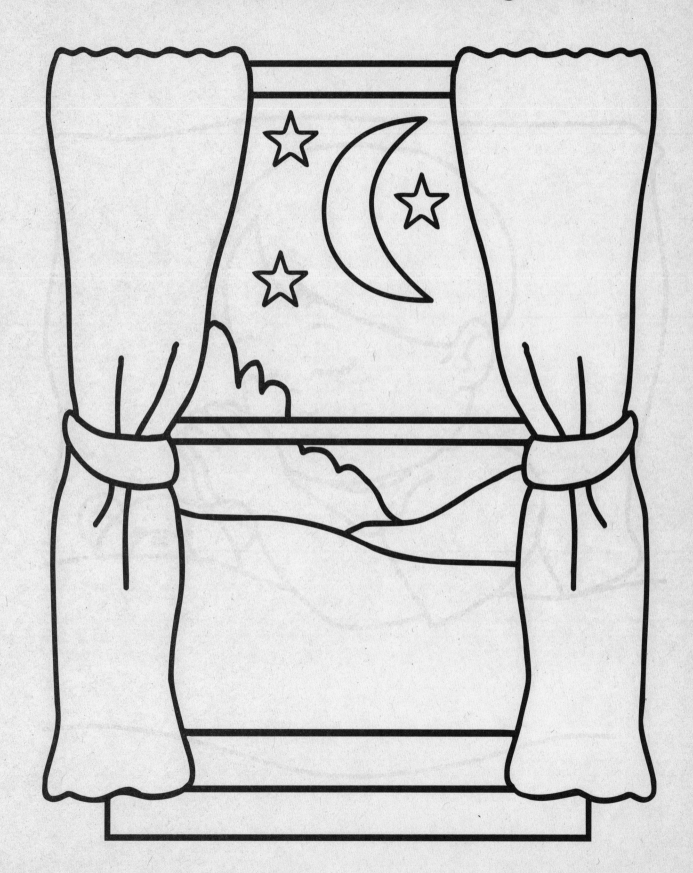

God cares for me when I am sleeping.

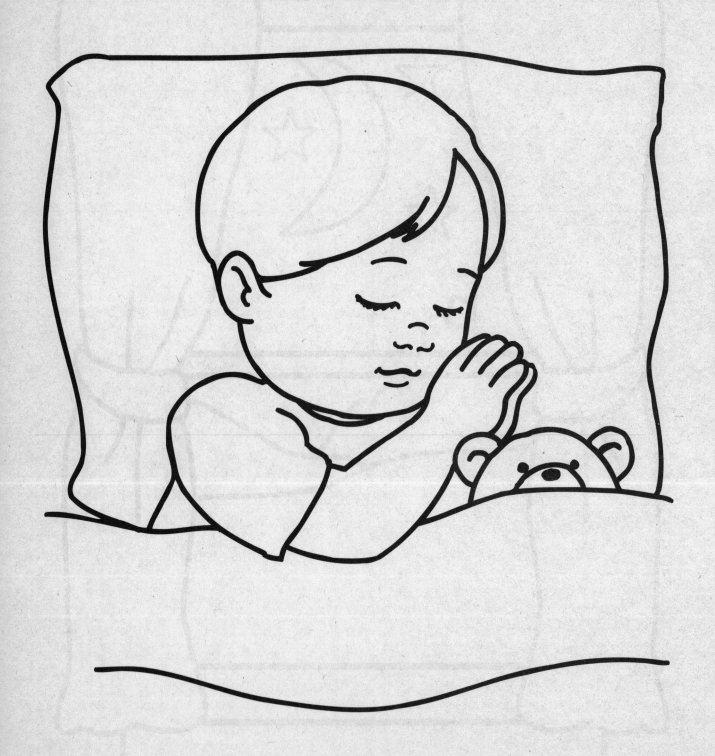

GOD CARES FOR ME

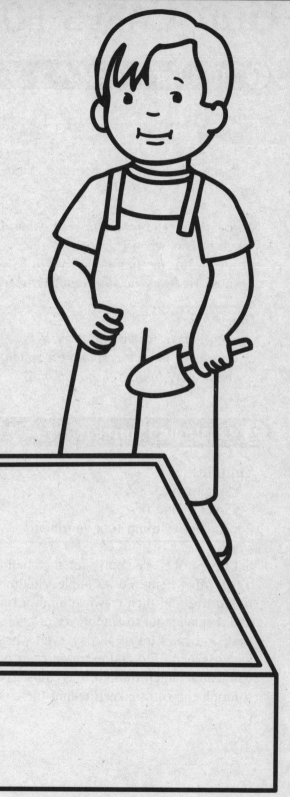

Supplies: Sandpaper, scissors, glue

Instructions: Before class, cut the pieces of sandpaper into smaller portions so it is easier for the children to handle. During class, help the children glue their pieces of sandpaper to the sandbox on the coloring page. Remind the kids that God cares for them even when they are playing.

GOD CARES FOR ME

① "God Cares for Me"

Supplies
- None

Sing the following song with the children, with the motions, to the tune of "Mary Had a Little Lamb."

God cares for me *(point to self)*, when I sleep, *(hands folded under head)*
When I sleep, when I sleep
God cares for me *(point self)* when I sleep *(hands under head)*
Because He loves me so. *(hands crossed on chest)*

Other Verses:
...when I wake *(yawn and stretch)*
...when I eat *(mimic eating with spoon)*
...when I play *(mimic throwing ball)*

② Obstacle Course

Supplies
- Small table
- Small riding toy
- Toddler crawling tube *(optional)*

Set up an obstacle course for the children, using the furniture you have in your room and a few other items. For example, children could crawl under the table, ride a few feet on a riding toy, and then crawl through a toddler tube *(optional)*. For older children, you could add a small stool to climb over or chairs to run around. Tell toddlers before you start that God cares for us all day, even when we are playing. God likes for us to play because we are having fun and exercising our bodies that He gave us. For younger toddlers, you can lead children through the course as a Follow the Leader game. While you are going through the course, keep telling the children what you are doing and what comes next.

③ Sleeping Out

Supplies
- Large blanket
- Small blankets or pillows
- Flashlight
- Pop-up tent *(optional)*

Before class, set up a pop-up tent or drape a blanket over some folding chairs to create a tent. Slightly dim lights in class. Give each child a small pillow or blanket and tell them they are going to have a sleep-out. Remind them that God cares for them and is watching over them, even when they are sleeping. Guide the children to the tent with your flashlight. Help everyone to get into the tent and to lie down with their pillows. Pray a good-night prayer together, remembering to thank God that He cares for us all the time. You could also sing a quiet version of "Jesus Loves Me," or another class favorite, before ending the campout.

④ Sunshine Sun Catcher

Supplies
- Yellow tissue paper
- Pen
- Scissors
- Clear adhesive covering
- Glue stick

Before class, trace and cut 4" circles from yellow tissue paper. Also cut out many large triangular sunrays of various sizes. Cut clear adhesive covering into 10" lengths. Then remove the backing and fold covering in half length wise, smoothing out the bubbles as much as possible. Cut the clear covering into 7" circles. Give each child a clear circle and a tissue paper circle. Help children glue, with a glue stick, the yellow circle into the middle of the clear circle. Children can then pick out some sun rays to glue around the edge of the yellow circle. This will create a sun to hang in a window and remind them that God cares for them when they wake up and all day long.

Jesus loves mothers.

Jesus loves fathers.

Jesus loves families.

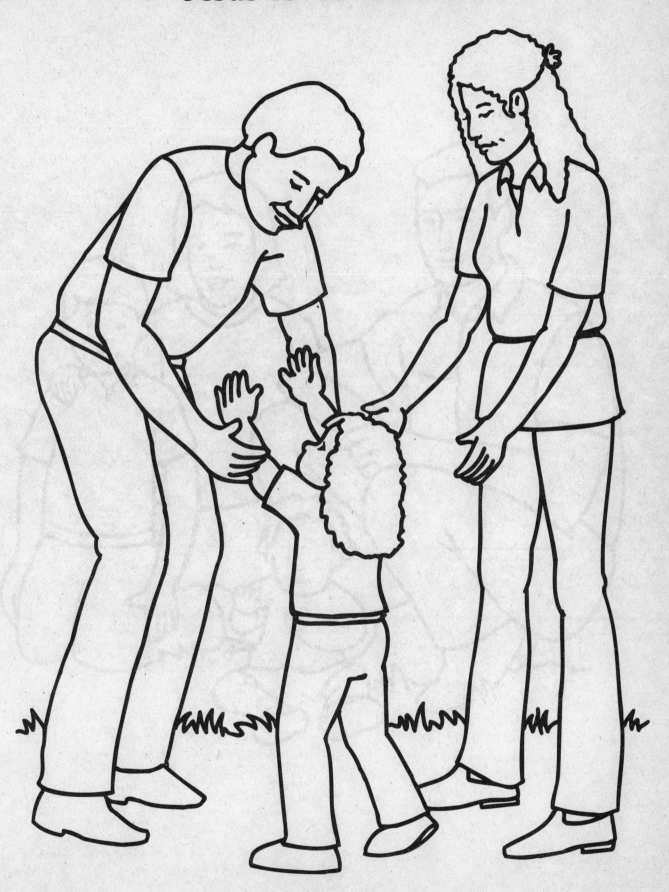

I love my family.

Jesus loves children.

Jesus loves children.

Jesus loves children.

Jesus loves children.

Jesus loves people.

Jesus loves people.

Jesus loves people.

Jesus loves people.

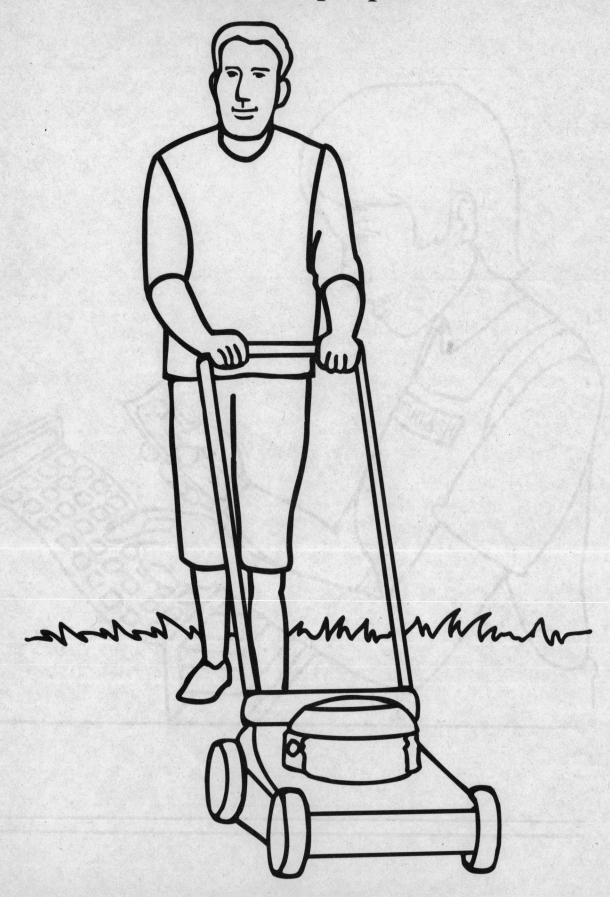

Jesus loves people.

Jesus loves you.

Jesus loves me.

Jesus Loves Me

Supplies: Foil, scissors, glue sticks

Instructions: Before class, cut pieces of foil into squares, rectangles, and ovals. During class, help the chilren glue foil, shiny side up, onto the mirror frames on their coloring pages. Help the kids press down on their foil pieces and then look into them and say "Jesus loves me."

JESUS LOVES ME

① Fingerprint Pictures

Supplies
- White paper
- Pen
- Washable ink pads
- Large crayons
- Moist towelettes

Before class, write "Jesus Loves _____" along the top of a white piece of paper, one per child. Draw a circle on each paper for the children to decorate as a face. As children get their papers at the table, write the child's name in the blank. Talk about how Jesus loves them and how each one of them is very special. Even their fingerprints are different! Then help children place their fingers on the washable ink pads and use their fingerprints to decorate the face on their paper. Help them make features and any other type of decoration. They can also use crayons to color their faces. When children are finished using the ink pads, wash the ink off their hands in a sink or with moist towelettes.

② The Jesus Loves Me Jump

Supplies
- Construction paper
- Pen
- Picture of Jesus
- Masking tape
- Markers
- Magazine *(optional)*

Before class, write "Jesus" in big letters on a piece of construction paper. Tape a picture of Jesus on the paper too. Write "Loves" on another piece of paper and draw a red heart. On the third piece of construction paper, write "Me" and draw picture of a child (or use one from a magazine). Tape these three pieces of paper to the floor, about 2' apart. Line up the children and ask them to jump over each piece of construction paper, one at a time. Older or more verbal children can say the word on the paper as they jump over it. For younger toddlers, the teacher can say the word while the toddler jumps or walks over it. After the child completes the three jumps, they can run back to the line and tag the next child. Continue until all children have a chance to jump.

③ "Jesus Loves Me"

Supplies
- None

Sing the following to the tune of "Old McDonald Had a Farm," doing the motions and encouraging the children to sing along.

Jesus loves me; yes, He does *(point to self)*
And He loves you too. *(point to others)*
Jesus loves me; yes, He does *(point to self)*
And He loves you too! *(point to others)*
(At this part, leader sings the names of individual children and points to them. Make sure to sing it enough times that all children are included.)
He loves Tanya, He loves Sam, He loves Jamal, and He loves Anisha! *(point to children as you name them)*

(All sing ending)
Jesus loves me; yes, He does *(point to self)*
And He loves you too! *(point to others)*

④ See Who Jesus Loves

Supplies
- Paper towel or toilet paper tubes, one for each child
- Stickers (Jesus stickers, if possible)
- Pictures of people *(optional)*

Give each child a tube and some stickers. Help them apply the stickers all over the tube. Teacher should have a tube too. Look through your tube and say, **Let's see who Jesus loves. Oh, I see Natasha. Jesus loves Natasha!** Have children look around the room for someone that Jesus loves. Encourage them to point the tubes to look at one another. If you have posters of various types of people on the wall, ask children to look at those to see more people that Jesus loves. You could also sit in a circle and ask children, one at a time, to look through the tube and see someone who Jesus loves. Help younger and less verbal children by naming for them the child at whom they are looking.

I sing at church.

I sing about Jesus.

I pray at church.

God hears me pray.

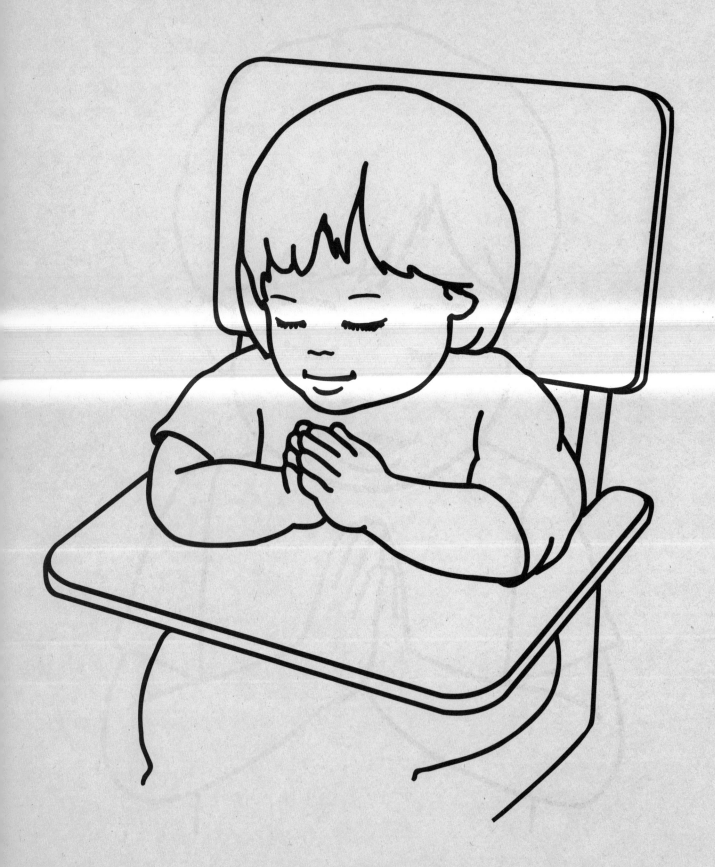

I learn at church.

I learn from my teacher.

I learn God loves me.

I learn about Jesus.

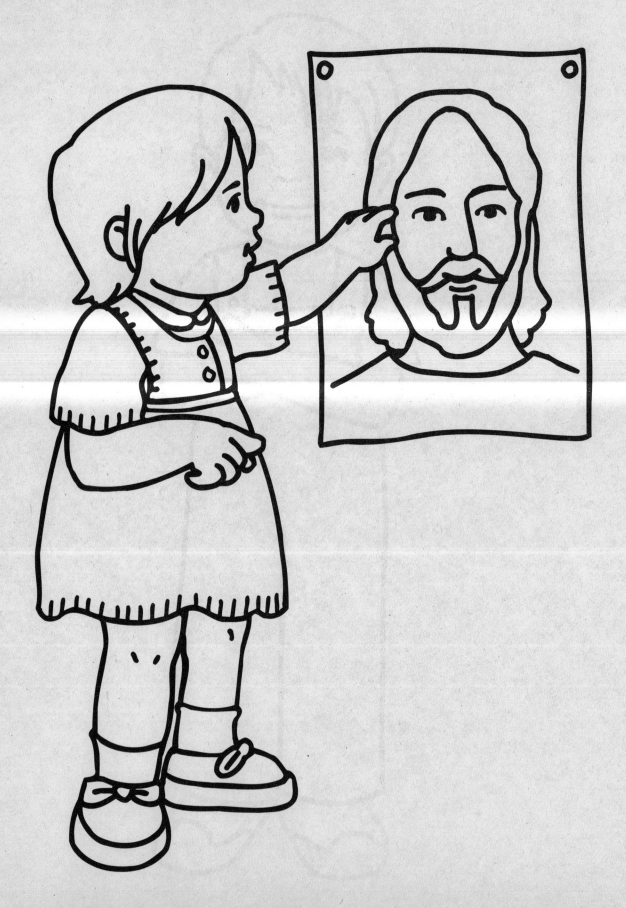

I have friends at church.

I am a friend to others.

God gives me friends.

I Go to Church

Supplies: Tissue paper (of various colors), glue sticks

Instructions: Before class, tear tissue paper into various small sizes and shapes. During class, let each child choose pieces of paper to glue onto the stained-glass windows of the church on the picture page. Allow the children to show the class the different colors they chose for their windows. Remind them that we all go to church to learn more about God.

MY CHURCH

① Going to Church

Supplies
- Small stuffed animal or baby doll for each child
- Children's Bible
- Blanket
- Crackers
- Paper plates

Spread a blanket in the corner of the room with a children's Bible, crackers, and paper plates nearby. Give each child a stuffed animal or doll and tell them to follow you and take their animals to church. When you get to the blanket, encourage everyone to sit down and to make their animals or dolls sit down too. Start off by singing a simple worship song together. Then read a story from the children's Bible, holding the book up so the children and their animals can see. Then have prayer time. Encourage everyone to fold their hands. Lastly, you can give each child a few crackers for snack time.

② Praise God Shakers

Supplies
- Paper lunch bags
- Large crayons
- Stickers of crosses, Bibles, Jesus, churches
- Oyster crackers
- Bowl
- Large spoons
- Tape
- CD player *(optional)*
- Worship music CD *(optional)*

Give each child a paper bag. Encourage them to make colorful designs on both sides of the bag. Write each child's name near the bottom of his bag. After they color, give children stickers to decorate their bags. Then, put a scoop of oyster crackers in each bag. Older children can hold the bag while you put the crackers inside. Fold down the bag a few times and tape it shut. Each child now has a shaker! Tell them they are going to sing like we always do at church because we want to praise God. Sing "Jesus Loves the Little Children" or a similar song and encourage them to sing and shake their bags. You could also play children's worship songs and have them sing along with their new shakers.

③ Finding Bibles

Supplies
- Small Bibles
- Construction paper
- Scissors
- Stickers of Jesus
- Tape

Before class, affix stickers of Jesus to small pieces of construction paper and tape inside the front covers of several small Bibles. Scatter the Bibles around in one part of the room. Bring the children over to the area and help each one find one Bible and hold it. When they all have Bibles, ask them to sit down with you in a circle. Tell them to open their Bibles and find Jesus in the Bible. Remind them that Jesus loves them very much. While they are holding the Bibles, you could also read to them a story from an illustrated Bible.

④ Sponge Ball

Supplies
- Plastic grocery bag
- Several clean, unused hand-size sponges

Before class, put all the sponges into your plastic grocery bag. In class, dump out all the sponges on the floor. Ask children to pick them up and help you stuff them into the plastic bag. Do not let the children hold the plastic bag. Tie a secure knot on the bag, tightening it so the sponges form a ball inside the bag. Remind them of the things we do at church—sing, pray, learn about Jesus, and play with our friends. Have children stand in a circle and practice throwing the sponge ball to one another. You could also kick the ball back and forth across the circle, making sure everyone has a turn to kick it. As an alternative for young toddlers, sit in a circle and pass the ball around while singing a song.

Noah was a good man.

God told Noah to build a big boat.

Noah worked hard.

Noah obeyed God.

Noah brought animals into the ark.

Noah brought two of every animal.

Noah brought big animals.

Noah brought small animals.

God sent rain.

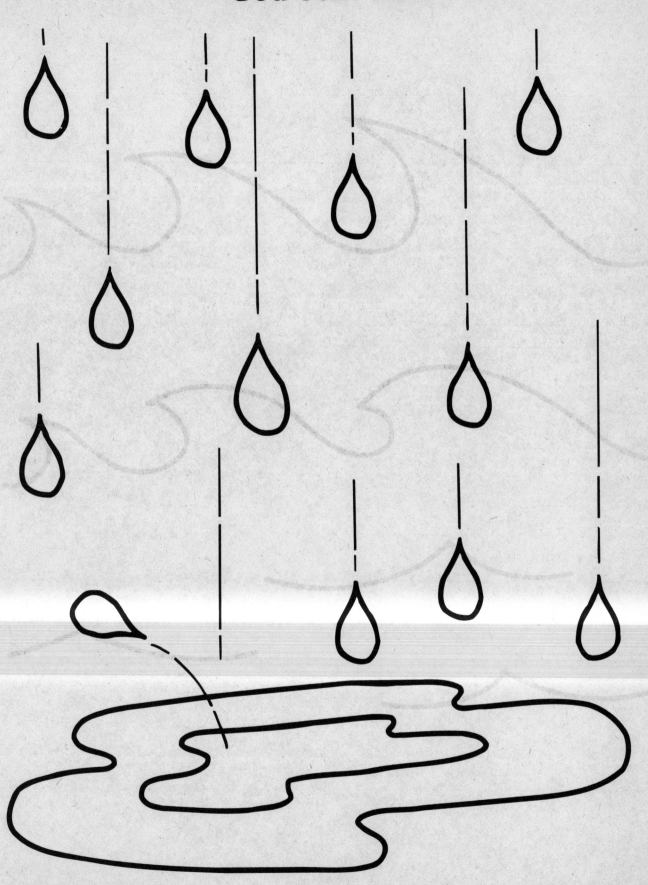

There was a flood.

The ark floated on the water.

The rain stopped.

God put a rainbow in the sky.

GOD MAKES A PROMISE

Supplies: Glue sticks, large crayons

Instructions: Tell the children to color their rainbows pretty colors. Explain to them that the rainbow was a sign of God's promise to Noah. Once they are done coloring, let each child choose a couple of jumbo cotton balls and help them glue the cotton onto the cloud shapes on their coloring pages. Remind them that God keeps His promises.

NOAH

1 Rainbow in a Bag

Supplies
- Water
- Three boxes colorful fruit gelatin, like blue, red, and yellow
- Small pan
- Wooden spoon
- Stove
- Three small bowls
- Heavy resealable plastic freezer bags
- Masking tape

Before class, prepare each gelatin separately. Chill each bowl in the refrigerator for about 20 minutes until partially set and thickened. Stir a few times during the 20 minutes. Take bowls out of refrigerator and leave out until class, not too long. Spoon three different colors into several different heavy resealable plastic freezer bags. The bags should not be too full. Zip the bags closed, double-bag them, and seal with masking tape to help prevent leaks. In class, give children the bags to squeeze and knead. Show them how the colors blend together in the bags to make a rainbow. Tell them how that reminds us of the rainbow God put in the sky when He promised Noah that He would never again flood the earth.

2 Rainmaker

Supplies
- Foam cups
- Sharpened pencil
- Crayons
- Unsharpened pencils
- Large plastic tub
- Water
- Towels

Before class, turn over foam cups and use a pencil to gently push the beginning of two small holes in the bottom of the cups. Before class, fill a large tub with water. Give each child a foam cup. The children will turn over the cups and make rainmakers by pushing an unsharpened pencil through the small holes. Younger children will need more help pushing the pencil through the cup. Take children to the tub of water and show them how their rainmakers work. Fill a cup and hold it over the tub, showing them how the rain came down. Remind them that for Noah, it rained for 40 days and nights.

③ Animal Sounds

Supplies

- A box with toy animals

In class, gather the children around the box of toy animals. Explain that you are showing them some of the animals that Noah took with him on the boat. When you hold one up, ask them to tell you the sound that animal makes. Hold up one at a time and help children if they don't know the sound it makes. Next, you can have each child pick one from the box, and everyone can imitate the sound that animal makes. In addition, every time you take out an animal, the children could show you how that animal walks. For example, the children could crawl around like dogs, barking too!

④ Building the Boat

Supplies

- Several brown paper grocery bags, at least 10
- Stack of newspaper
- Masking tape
- Toy hammers, saws, and other tools
- Wooden blocks
- Fine sandpaper

Before class, stuff 10 or more brown grocery bags with crumpled newspaper, about halfway full. Fold over the top of the bags and secure with masking tape. These are the pieces of "wood" children can use to build a boat. In class, give children each some kind of tool and tell them to help you build the boat. You can guide them into lining up the grocery bags and making a boat outline. Allow them to hammer and saw the "wood." You could also give them wooden blocks on which to hammer and saw. Other children can use the sandpaper to sand the blocks. Talk about how Noah obeyed God and spent a lot of time building the boat.

Joseph and Mary were married.

Mary was Jesus' mother.

Jesus was born.

Jesus is God's Son.

Angels sang the night Jesus was born.

Shepherds came to visit Jesus.

The shepherds were happy Jesus was born.

Wise men saw a star.

The star led the wise men to Jesus.

The wise men gave Jesus gifts.

BABY JESUS WAS BORN

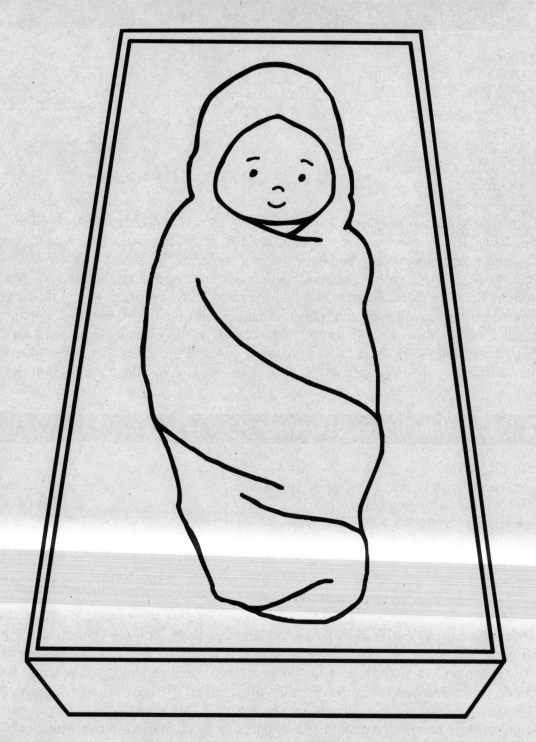

Supplies: Long strips of hay, strips of yellow paper, or wide raffia glue sticks

Instructions: While children are seated at the table, have them choose some materials to use as the hay in baby Jesus' manger. Once they have their hay, help each child glue it onto the manger on their coloring pages. Remind the children that Jesus was a baby, just like they once were.

BABY JESUS

① Following the Star

Supplies
- Yellow or white cardstock or construction paper
- Scissors
- Glitter
- Glue
- Flashlights
- Child-safe nativity set
- Yarn

Before class, cut star shapes out of yellow or white paper and decorate with glitter. Make one larger star to represent the star that was over baby Jesus. Attach stars to yarn and suspend from ceiling. Hang the larger star in a corner of the room above the child-safe nativity set. In class, gather children together and hand each a small flashlight. Tell them you are going to follow the star and find the baby Jesus. Tell them to aim their flashlights at the stars, which should sparkle when the light hits them. Dim the lights and walk around the classroom on a "journey." Talk about how the wise men followed a star to find baby Jesus. Tell the children to find the larger star and then, together, follow the large star to stand by the child-safe nativity set. Show the children the baby Jesus in the manger. Sing "Away in a Manger."

② Peek-a-boo Boxes

Supplies
- Several small boxes, shoe-box size or smaller
- Christmas wrapping paper
- Scissors
- Tape
- Bows
- Several small items relating to Jesus' birth, like baby Jesus doll, toy donkey, manger, hay, piece of cloth, angel doll, star

Before class, wrap several small boxes and lids, separately, with Christmas paper. Put bows atop the lids. Inside each box, place an item that relates to the story of Jesus' birth, like hay, a star, a piece of cloth, or a toy donkey. In class, tell children you are going to look inside the Peek-a-boo Boxes. Have a child open one of the boxes and peek inside. Ask *What do you see?* If the child sees hay, for example, talk about how Jesus was born in a place where animals lived and hay was probably all around. Continue with all children until each one has had a chance to peek inside a box and talk about what they see.

③ Pencil Holder Gifts

Supplies
- Clean, empty, plastic frozen juice containers (one for each child)
- Construction paper
- Tape or glue sticks
- Stickers
- Marker

Before class, the teacher should cover each juice container with construction paper so that the label is covered. Tell the children they are going to make gifts to give to someone in their family to celebrate Jesus' birth. Tell them Jesus was God's gift to us, and it is fun to give gifts to others. Give each child an empty container and tell them to choose stickers to decorate it. Once they've finished decorating, the teacher should write on the pencil holder: "This is a gift from:_____."

④ Christmas Card Puzzles

Supplies
- Several Christmas cards with pictures relating to Jesus' birth
- Clear adhesive covering
- Scissors

Before class, gather Christmas cards that have pictures of baby Jesus, Mary and Joseph, the stable, manger, angels, shepherds, and the wise men. Cut off the front of the cards and cover with clear adhesive covering. Cut each card in half, curving each cut to look like a puzzle piece. With the children, scatter the card pieces around on the floor or table. (You should only use two or three puzzles at the same time.) Ask the children to help you match the halves together, like putting together a puzzle. As the children fit together the cards, ask them about the picture they've made. Talk about that part of the Christmas story and then continue with another card. For older children, you could cut each card into four pieces to make it more challenging.

Jesus' Birth

Jesus' Resurrection

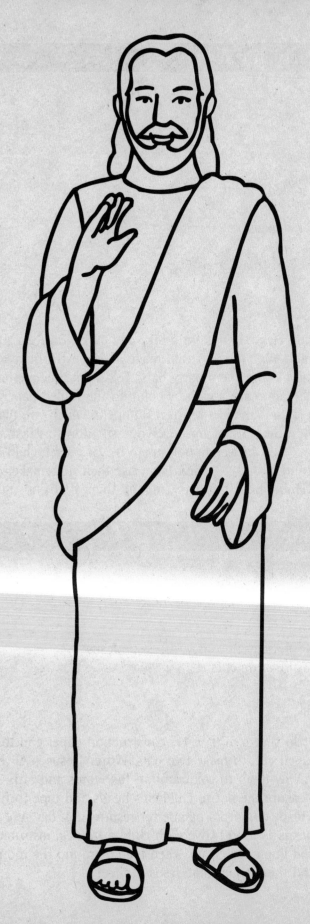

SPECIAL DAYS

① Birthday Party for Jesus

Supplies
- Red and green streamers
- Colorful balloons
- Party hats
- Tape
- Colored paper, folded in half
- Large crayons
- Nativity and star stickers
- CD player
- CD of children's Christmas carols
- Noisemakers
- Cupcakes

Before class, decorate classroom as for a birthday party. Tape up streamers and balloons (out of reach of children), and you could make a "Happy Birthday Jesus" sign to display. When children come in, give them party hats. Tell them they are having a birthday party for Jesus. Each child can make a card by coloring the folded paper and putting stickers inside. You could play a game like Musical Bumps in which you play carols and children jump or dance. When the music stops, everyone sits down as fast as they can. At snack time, pray and thank God for sending Jesus to us. Give each child a noisemaker and sing a happy birthday song to Jesus, letting them use their noisemakers. Then give each child a birthday cupcake. Throughout the party, remind them that Christmas is Jesus' birthday.

② Easter Parade

Supplies
- White or pastel construction paper
- Tape
- Crayons
- Easter stickers, especially flowers, crosses, or Jesus
- Children's musical instruments
- CD player
- Children's praise CD

Before class, tape two sheets of 8" x 11" construction paper end to end. Cut the papers length-wise, using a scalloped cut, to make two hats. Write, "Jesus is Alive" on the papers. Give each child a paper and allow them to color around the words and affix stickers all over the hat, the more the better. Measure the hat to children's heads and tape to fit. Tell children to put on their hats and get ready to have a parade for resurrection day. **We are praising God and celebrating that Jesus is alive!** Give each child a musical instrument to play in the parade. Play a praise CD and line children up. Then march around the room, playing the instruments and singing. Remind them again that Jesus is alive!

HeartShaper® Toddlers & 2s Scope & Sequence

Fall

Winter

Spring

Summer